Drawing Fun Fashions

SKATER CHIC *Style*

FUN FASHIONS YOU CAN SKETCH

By **Mari Bolte**   illustrated by **Jennifer Rzasa**

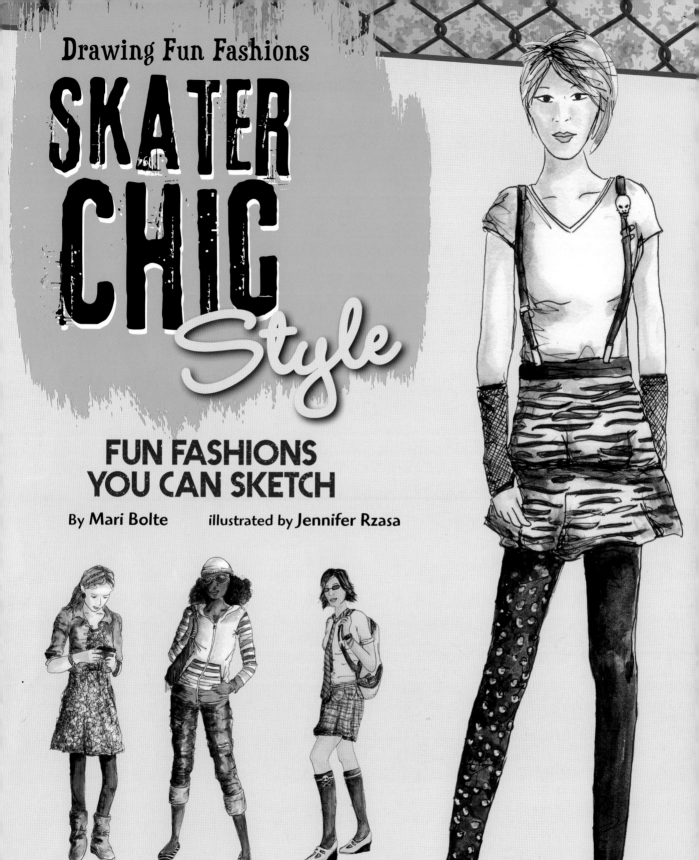

CAPSTONE PRESS
a capstone imprint

Snap books

TABLE OF CONTENTS

The first skateboard was built in the late 1950s. Since then, skater girls have brought their own senses of style to the sport. Skater girls aren't afraid to update their wardrobes. Bling, bright colors, and animal prints make everyday clothing skater chic.

Each outfit shows step-by-step instructions on how to draw your very own fashion model. Build upon simple shapes, and use erasable guidelines to create a human shape.

STEP 1: Start with a simple line drawing. Pick your favorite pose, and use light guidelines to build your model.

TIP: Skaters don't stand still, so why should your sketches? Try drawing your models in action perfecting ollies, nailing kickflips, and grinding across the skate park.

STEP 2: Darken the outlines, and start adding in details like hemlines and hand placements.

STEP 3: Erase guidelines, and draw in things like fabric prints, hair, facial features, and accessories.

TIP: Ink pens and watercolor pencils and paints will give you the distressed look of the art in this book.

STEP 4: Finish any final details and then add in color, textures, and shading to bring your model to life.

Back to Basics

Start simple with blue jeans and layered tanks. Stick to relaxed fit clothing and sensible accessories. The skater chic style is all about being comfortable in what you wear.

TIP: Use shading to add creases and depth to the shirts and pants.

VERT STYLE

A trucker hat, boyfriend sweater, and awesome jeans are all you need to reach the height of skater chic.

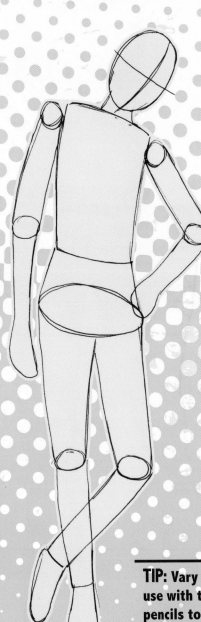

TIP: Vary the pressure you use with the watercolor pencils to create the look of these one-of-a-kind jeans.

Punk
You Out

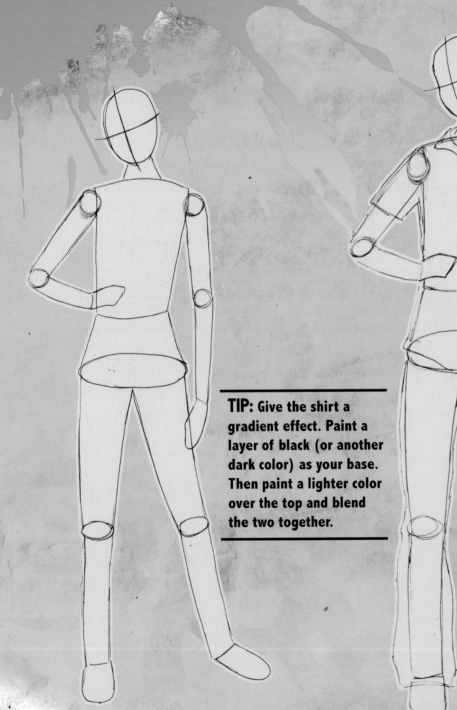

TIP: Give the shirt a gradient effect. Paint a layer of black (or another dark color) as your base. Then paint a lighter color over the top and blend the two together.

Skater girls are relaxed and low maintenance. Go with the flow in short-sleeved plaid, and relaxed-fit jeans. And a messenger bag that holds any accessory is just what a serious skater needs.

STREET LEAGUE STYLE

The skater boy is as casual as they come. He's ready to hang with friends on the sidelines or gain big air in a halfpipe. Fashion stays on the down-low with street league style.

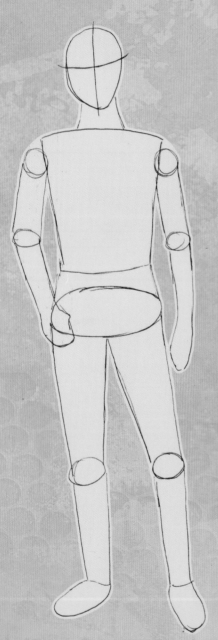

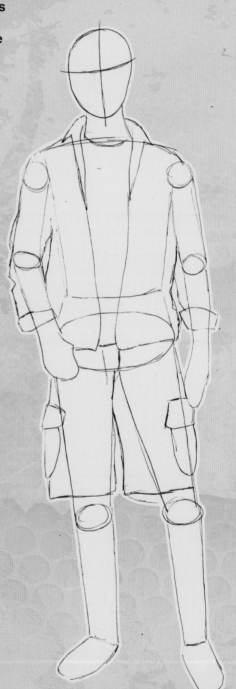

TIP: Plaid is a great pattern for experimenting with color. Try color combinations that you haven't used before.

SKATER PREP

Educate yourself at skater school while looking stylish too. Put a spin on ordinary plaid by adding an underlayer of taffeta and an overlayer of silver chains.

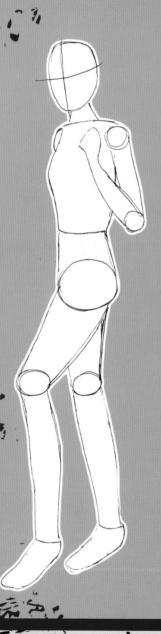

TIP: Try using a cotton swab to soften the lines for a more natural look. Moisten the cotton swab for a more blended pattern.

SURF SKATER

When skater girls need sun, they hit the beach and surf the boardwalk! Wave to the crowd in style while wearing natural tones of the earth and sea.

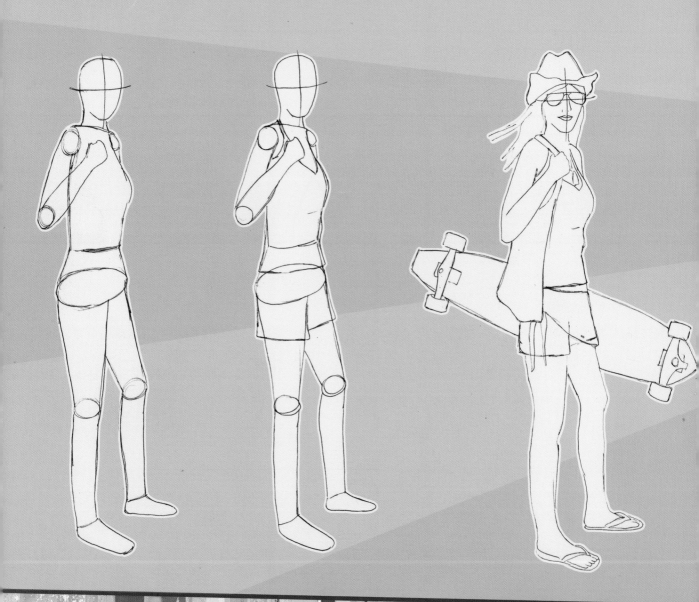

TIP: Keep your pencil lines short and jagged. This will give your sketch a more rugged feel.

Hanging with the Homies

Get relaxed with skater chic casual wear. Dress up familiar jeans with a super stylish hoodie. Add coordinating sunglasses and a tasseled bag. Then top things off with a knit hat. Hanging out never looked so good!

TIP: Use both white and dark gray paints to add shading and dimension to the distressed jeans.

STANDING OUT IN THE SKATE TRAFFIC

Get wild with animal print! Limiting the print to accessories ensures that your eyes won't be overpowered. A fierce hat, bag, and pair of shoes will get you noticed in even the heaviest of skate traffic.

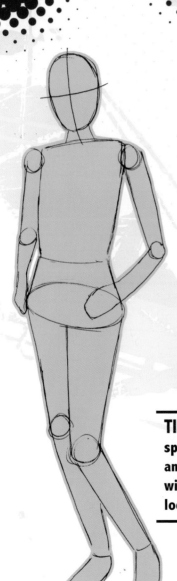

TIP: Make sure the leopard spots are different sizes and shapes. This difference will help make the pattern look more natural.

TOP DECK STYLE

Skater guys have a sense of style too! Keep it simple with casual pants and a tee. Give the outfit a personal twist with a colorful coat, a pair of shoes, and a bright belt.

TIP: With its simple lines, this outfit can be tailored to fit your own personal style.

Overall Impression

Skater girls don't spend all day at the skate park. For more dressy occasions, a sundress, boots, and denim jacket will take the stylish skater anywhere she pleases.

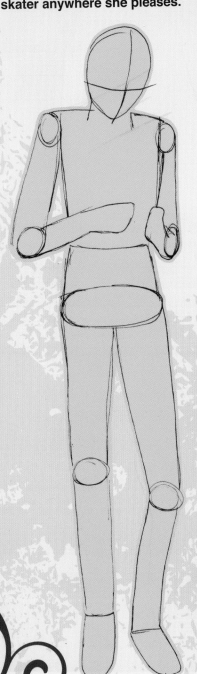

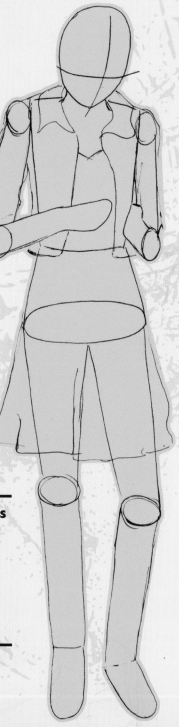

TIP: Use watercolor pencils to create the dress print. Color in the pattern, and then brush gently with a wet paintbrush. Once the pattern is dry, use a black pen to add more texture.

TIP: Try using the watercolor pencils on a wet surface. See which technique you like better.

Supertech Sparkle

Get ready to go out by adding a shimmery sparkle. Start with an animal print skirt as a centerpiece. Then add a few pieces of interest that catch the eye.

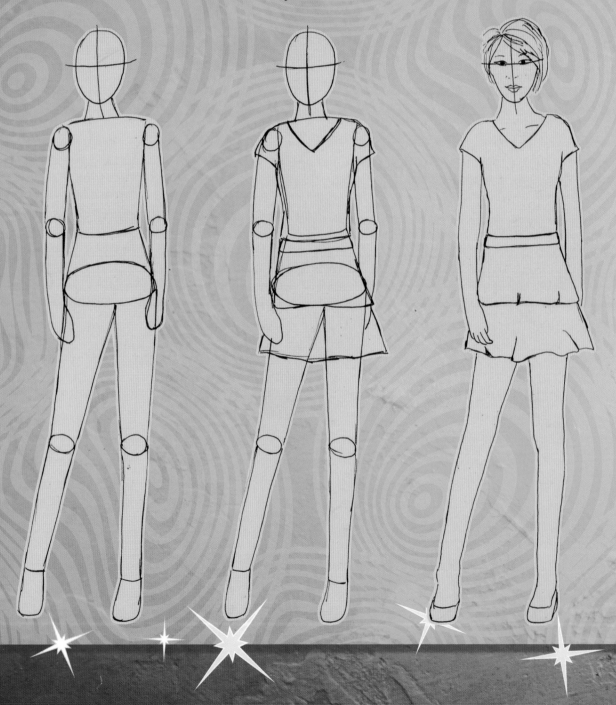

TIP: Experiment with texture! Glue down a piece of fabric in place of the skirt. Or use glitter glue for some 3-D shine.

1080 Winter Wear

Staying warm while rolling through snow is important. Looking good while doing it is important too! Turn heads on the hill with gear that's snowboarder chic.

TIP: Practice creating cool graphics using paint and markers. Snowboards are great canvases for street-inspired art.

At the PARK

Dress to impress at the skate park! Hi-top boots, a practical-but-fashionable outfit, and a helmet will get you noticed. Grab a board and you're ready to go.

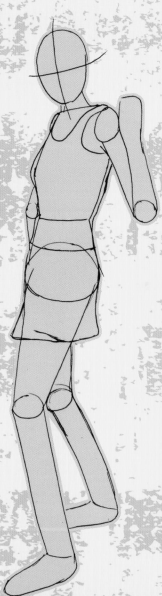

TIP: Turn safety gear into an accessory! Coordinate outfits with helmets, goggles, gloves, and protective pads.

EXTRA ACCESSORIES

Use your creativity to create original accessories for each outfit. Each piece will reflect your personal style and taste! Take your time and figure out what works for you. Don't be afraid to be extreme!

TIP: Skater style isn't just a fashion statement—some people live the skate life. Skaters like to show off their sport wherever they go. There is never a shortage of cool accessories to draw!

TIP: Get inspired! Check out punk and hip-hop labels to find more ideas for skater chic accessories.

READ MORE

Guillain, Charlotte. *Punk: Music, Fashion, Attitude!* Culture in Action. Chicago: Raintree, 2011.

Torres, Laura. *Rock your Wardrobe.* QEB Rock Your … Irvine, CA.: QEB Pub., 2010.

Wooster, Patricia. *Fashion Designer.* Cool Arts Careers. Ann Arbor, Mich.: Cherry Lake Pub., 2012.

INTERNET SITES

FactHound offers a safe, fun way to find Internet sites related to this book. All of the sites on FactHound have been researched by our staff.

Here's all you do:

Visit *www.facthound.com*

Type in this code: 9781620650387

 Super-cool stuff!   Check out projects, games and lots more at **www.capstonekids.com**

Snap Books are published by Capstone Press,
1710 Roe Crest Drive, North Mankato, Minnesota 56003
www.capstonepub.com

Library of Congress Cataloging-in-Publication Data
Bolte, Mari.
  Skater chic style : fun fashions you can sketch / by Mari Bolte.
    pages cm. — (Snap. Drawing fun fashions)
  Summary: "Lively text and fun illustrations describe how to draw cool fashions"—Provided by publisher.
  ISBN 978-1-62065-038-7 (library binding)
  ISBN 978-1-4765-1786-5 (ebook PDF)
1. Fashion drawing—Juvenile literature. 2. Skaters—Clothing—Juvenile literature. I. Title.
  TT509.B6545 2013
  741.6'72—dc23   2012028473

Editorial Credits
Lori Bye, designer; Nathan Gassman, art director; Marcie Spence, media researcher;
Laura Manthe, production specialist

The illustrations in this book were created with watercolors and ink.
Design elements by Shutterstock.

Printed in the United States of America in North Mankato, Minnesota.
092012   006933CGS13